Elissa and the Stone

Story by Julie Mitchell
Illustrations by Amanda Dawson

NELSON
A Cengage Company

Elissa and the Stone

Text: Julie Mitchell
Illustrations: Amanda Dawson
Editor: Katrina Wilson
Design: Goanna Graphics (Vic) Pty Ltd
Reprint: Siew Han Ong

PM Plus
Sapphire Level 30

ISBN 978 0 17 010814 0
ISBN 978 0 17 010812 6 (set)

Cengage Learning Australia
Level 5 , 80 Dorcas Street
Southbank VIC 3006
Phone: 1300 790 853
Email: aust.nelsonprimary@cengage.com

For learning solutions, visit cengage.com.au

Printed in China by 1010 Printing International Ltd
30 23

Contents

Chapter 1
Phobia

"It's a great speech," Joel said. "It's just a shame no one else is going to get to hear it."

Elissa frowned at her twin. "What do you mean?"

"Well," Joel continued, "it's one thing to make a speech in front of your brother, but it's another to make it in front of all of Year Eight." He paused, looking serious. "Have you forgotten what happened the last time you tried to say something in front of an audience?"

She had, of course. But now the memory sprang up like some hideous jack-in-the-box. There she was, dressed as a villager in last year's school play. The Pied Piper was beginning to draw the children of Hamelin away with his music, and she knew it was almost time to step forward and say her line. As she waited, she glanced at the audience – there were so many people out there, watching and listening to everything. If she made a mistake, they would know … every one of them would know. And she would die of embarrassment.

Her heart thumped in her chest, and her stomach trembled. Then she heard the piper play the run of notes that was her cue. She tried to move, but her feet seemed bolted to the stage. One of the other villagers gave her a shove, and she stumbled forward.

The piper stopped playing. Elissa was supposed to say, "Where are you taking the children?" But something was terribly wrong with her throat. When she tried to speak, it locked up so tightly that nothing came out. Again and again, she tried to say her line, but her voice remained trapped inside.

The silence was awful. It went on for so long that the piper finally said, "I suppose you're wondering where I'm taking the children."

She managed to nod and, mercifully, a short time later, the curtain fell.

"Liss?" Joel said, bringing her back to the present. "I didn't mean to upset you. I think you'd make a great student council representative."

"Well, we'll never know," Elissa said, blinking back tears, "because you're right – there's no way I can make a speech in front of everyone. And without a speech, I don't stand a chance of being elected." She ran upstairs to her room.

What a waste of good ideas, she thought, tossing her speech in the bin. New books for the library ... up-to-date computer software ... an afterschool activities program ...

They were all good ideas, but she wouldn't be able to develop them further. And why not? Because she was afraid of speaking in public. Afraid she would be embarrassed again.

Fresh tears threatened, and Elissa knew she had to think about something else. She changed into her pyjamas, curled up under her doona, and began deliberately studying the wallpaper.

On a beige background, golden leaves wound themselves around vertical golden stripes. Elissa examined each stripe in turn, trying to spot a flaw in the pattern. And on the twelfth stripe from the corner, she found one – the leaves on this stripe were shinier, and slightly green. She moved on to the thirteenth stripe, and found another fault – the stripe was brown and the leaves were a glossy dark green.

Her eyelids grew heavy with the strain, and her body began to relax. Moments later, she discovered an amazing thing – the wallpaper didn't seem like wallpaper at all any more. It had become a dense green jungle of bushes and vines.

"Helps!" cried a voice somewhere in the distance. "Please, helps me!"

Elissa fought her way through the tangled plant growth.

"Helps!" the voice cried again. And now, just ahead, Elissa could see its owner.

The little man was definitely in trouble. He was stuck, upside down, in a thorn bush, his helmet covering his eyes and his feet poking out in the air. He looked like a human cannonball that had missed its target.

"Don't move!" Elissa called, running over to the little man. "You're in a thorn bush, and if you struggle, you'll get ripped to pieces." She knelt beside him, reached carefully through the branches, and pushed back his helmet so that he could see.

The man blinked, stared at her with his bright blue eyes, then drew his shaggy brows together in a frown. "I knows I's in a thorn bush," he said. "I can tell by the way I's being prickded and pokeded. Can you sees my sword anywhere?"

Elissa checked the ground underneath the bush. "Is this what you mean?" she asked, plucking something that looked very much like a kitchen knife from the undergrowth.

"Yes," the man said. "You can use it to cuts away some of the thorns. Then I'll be able to gets myself down."

"I won't need to do any cutting," Elissa said, pointing to a branch. "When I pull this away, you can push off sideways and get free." She lay down the knife, and carefully took hold of the branch. "By the way," she added, "my name's Elissa. What's yours?"

"Shale," the little man said, watching her bend back the bough.

"Time to jump, Shale," Elissa said.

Shale tumbled out of the bush, almost knocking Elissa over. Then he got to his feet and brushed himself down. He was no taller than her shoulder, and close inspection revealed that his helmet was actually a pudding basin with a strap. He wore a flannel shirt tucked into a pair of baggy pants. The pants were stuffed into patched rubber boots, and his whole outfit was set off by a belt of knotted rope.

"What kind of soldier are you, Shale?" Elissa asked. "I don't think I've seen that particular uniform before."

Shale blushed, then straightened his shoulders. "I isn't a soldier," he said huffily. "I's a farmer. And if it wasn't for that scoundrel, Ashakhan, I wouldn't be nearly getsing myself killded in this war!"

"War?" Elissa said. "I don't see – or hear – any war going on."

Shale rolled his eyes. "Of course you doesn't. We's too far away. Which reminds me – where's my sword?"

Elissa picked up the kitchen knife and passed it to him.

"I thanks you," Shale said, slipping it into his belt. "Now I's ready to get back to the fightsing." With that, he marched off through the jungle.

Elissa suddenly feared for Shale. He was so little, and so ill-equipped, that he could never be a match for a serious opponent. "Wait," she called after him. "You haven't told me who this Ashakhan person is, or what the war's all about."

"I doesn't have time to talks," Shale said, "unless you wants to walk with me."

"Fine," Elissa said. Maybe she'd be able to talk him out of going back to the war if she tagged along.

Shale led the way, hacking at bushes and vines with his knife. It was hard work, since the knife was quite blunt, and he was exhausted by the time they broke clear of the jungle.

"Let's rest awhile," Elissa suggested.

Shale agreed. He dropped onto a log, took a flask of water from one pocket of his trousers, and passed it to her.

"Thanks," Elissa said, sitting beside him. She drank, and passed the bottle back. "Who's Ashakhan?" she asked, watching Shale drink.

The little man scowled. Then he wiped his lips, capped the flask, and returned it to his pocket. "Ashakhan," he said, "is a greedy thief. He takeses what he wants. Right now, what he wants is all the land in our valley. But people don't usually fights back when Ashakhan demandses their land."

"Why not?"

"Because he doesn't fights fair. First, he burnses their homes. And if they stays around, he sends his soldiers to deals with them. If that doesn't works ..." Shale paused, shuddering, "... then he comes out of his fortress and makeses things so bad that people just gives up and runs away."

"Sounds sensible to me," Elissa commented. "Is that what you were doing in the jungle? Running away?"

"No!" Shale cried. "I was fightsing! All of us farmers were fightsing the soldiers. Then Ashakhan came ridesing towards us, chanting and singing. He raised his arm, pointsing at us. And the next thing we knows, we's being blowed off our feet by a hurricane."

"And that's how you finished up in a thorn bush," Elissa said. Her brow wrinkled. "What is this guy? A wizard, or something?"

"No. He's just lucky. A long time ago, the mountain dwarves digged up an evil stone. They cursed it, and throwed it away. Ashakhan went looksing for it, and one day he found it." Shale sighed heavily. "He's been using its power to gets whatever he wants ever since."

"Do you know where he keeps the stone?"

"People say he keepses it in a special room in his fortress."

"Then that's where we're going," Elissa said. "We have to find that stone and destroy it."

"I can leads you to Ashakhan's fortress," Shale said, "but I can't touches the stone."

"Why not?" Elissa asked.

Shale shrugged. "I's a dwarf, and dwarves cursed it. If I gets too close, it'll kills me."

"Then I'll destroy the stone for you. Now, let's get going."

Shale led Elissa beyond the jungle to the bank of a wide river. "Sees those stepping stones?" he said, pointing upstream. "That's where we crosses. But we has to be quick, and we has to be quiet. We doesn't wants the crocodiles to notice us."

Elissa gasped. "Crocodiles? Where?"

"Over there," Shale said, pointing out two reptiles lying on the far bank. He put a finger to his lips in a gesture of silence, and walked a little way upstream. Then he began to cross the slow-moving river.

Elissa followed him out onto the stepping stones. They were set a short distance apart, and they were slippery. When she reached the third stone, she looked up and saw Shale leaping from one stone to the next, his helmet glinting in the sun. Then she glanced at the crocodiles – they seemed to be watching Shale with interest. She kept going, and didn't look up again until she was about halfway across the river. By then, Shale had almost reached the other side.

Elissa didn't see Shale slip, but she heard his cry, and the splash, as he fell into the water. And she saw the crocodiles slither into the river after him.

"Swim!" she screamed. But the little man didn't seem to understand. He slapped at the water for a second or two, then disappeared beneath it.

There was no time to waste! If Elissa didn't reach Shale soon, he would drown – or be taken by the crocodiles. She dived into the river and swam to him. Then, grasping one of his hands, she pulled him to the surface. He came up, spluttering and coughing, and she towed him towards the riverbank.

The crocodiles followed close behind, snapping their jaws. But when Elissa finally dragged Shale clear of the river, they lost interest, and slipped soundlessly beneath the water.

Shale coughed until his lungs were clear, then he turned to Elissa. "I thanks you again," he said. "You saveded my life."

"You're welcome," Elissa said. "Now, let's get out of here."

Some time later, the travellers crested a hill. And there, below them, lay Ashakhan's fortress.

"I doesn't see any guards," Shale said.

"Nor do I," Elissa said, "but I don't see any way to get in, either."

"We needs a closer look. Follow me."

Together, they descended the hill, hiding where they could among the few stunted trees that grew on it. Then they began to circle the fortress, looking for any opening in its sheer dark walls.

"There," Shale said suddenly, pointing.

Elissa strained her eyes. "I don't see anything but a wall."

"Looks closely," Shale said. "You sees that funny mark on the rock?"

"Yes."

"That shows it's a dwarfish door."

"Can you open it?"

Shale grinned at her, then he looked back at the door. "*Brihath*," he said.

The rock parted, and Shale led Elissa through the gap in the wall. "*Brihath*," he said once more, and the rock closed seamlessly behind them.

They found themselves in a passage lit by torches bracketed to the walls. Elissa took one of the torches and crept along the passage. Shale gasped as chamber after chamber revealed evidence of Ashakhan's astounding greed – treasure beyond price, and much of it stolen from dwarves. But it wasn't until the pair came upon a small room at the end of the passage that they found what they were looking for. Here, in the centre of the room, resting on a cushion, was a murky green stone about the size of an ostrich egg.

Shale froze in the doorway. “I can’t goes inside the room. You has to take the stone and smashes it.”

Elissa moved forward and studied the stone carefully. Then she reached towards it.

She was almost touching it when a snake rose in front of her.

Elissa snatched her hand away from the stone. Her heart was racing, but she backed off slowly, her eyes never leaving the hooded yellow-brown serpent.

"Don't fears it," Shale said from behind her. "It's blind, and it won't bites you unless it thinks you're afraid."

Shale's matter-of-fact tone made Elissa suspicious. "You *knew* about the snake!" she accused. "You knew and you didn't tell me."

"I confesses I did," Shale said, "but I didn't mentions it because that would've scared you. And if you were afraid, you couldn't have taken the stone. This isn't an ordinary snake. It's something Ashakhan maked with the stone. You has to gets past it without any fear."

"That's impossible!" Elissa wailed.

"Is it?" Shale asked. "You weren't afraid of the crocodiles when you dived into the river."

"I wasn't thinking about them. I was busy trying to save your life."

"Then don't thinks about the snake. Thinks about the lives you can save if you destroys the stone."

Elissa glanced over her shoulder at Shale. She looked back at the snake, then beyond it, to the stone. Her heartbeat slowed a little. And she took a step forward.

"That's it," Shale said. "Concentrates on the result. Thinks about the goal."

Elissa moved closer to the stone, ignoring the blind snake weaving back and forth in front of it.

"Thinks about the goal," Shale repeated as Elissa reached forward and grasped the stone.

Elissa pictured Shale and all of his friends free to work their farms in peace once more. She kept the vision before her and, as her heartbeat returned to normal, she took the stone from its resting place. Then she raised it high into the air, and smashed it on the floor.

Suddenly, exhaustion flooded through her, and she let herself collapse among the scattered fragments of stone. Shale's bright blue eyes were the last thing she saw before she fell asleep.

Elissa would have slept on and on, if it hadn't been for the voice: "Liss, wake up. It's time to get ready for school."

She woke up, and found herself in the familiar territory of her room. The whole thing had been a dream! "What time is it?" she asked Joel.

"Seven o'clock."

Elissa smiled. There was plenty of time to practise her election speech before school.

Later that morning, Elissa took her place on stage with the other Year Eight candidates. But when she stepped up to the microphone, her old fears returned. What if she made a mistake? What if her voice froze in her throat?

She closed her eyes and heard Shale's voice in her head: "Thinks about the goal."

It was easy after that. She simply thought about the things she would work towards if she were voted onto the student council. Then she pictured them coming true. She imagined new books arriving for the library, new software being loaded into the computers, and her friends and herself choosing which afterschool activities they might like to try.

As she opened her mouth to speak, she kept those images in her mind. Her voice did not fail her; instead, it rang out with such conviction that the audience cheered.

Afterwards, Joel sought Elissa out. "I'm so proud of you," he said, giving her a hug. "I'm sure you'll get voted onto the Student Council."

"I hope so," Elissa told her twin, "but I'll be okay if I don't. I already feel like a winner!"